Running Free

Sue Leather & Julian Thomlinson

Series Editor: Rob Waring
Story Editor: Julian Thomlinson
Series Development Editor: Sue Leather

HEINLE
CENGAGE Learning

Australia • Brazil • Japan • Korea • Mexico • Singapore • Spain • United Kingdom • United States

HEINLE
CENGAGE Learning

Page Turners Reading Library

Running Free
Sue Leather & Julian Thomlinson

Publisher: Andrew Robinson

Executive Editor: Sean Bermingham

Senior Development Editor:
Derek Mackrell

Assistant Editor: Sarah Tan

Director of Global Marketing:
Ian Martin

Content Project Manager:
Tan Jin Hock

Print Buyer:
Susan Spencer

Layout Design and Illustrations:
Redbean Design Pte Ltd

Cover Illustration: Eric Foenander

Photo Credits:
41–45 (bottom right corner)
occasionallyxxx/Deviantart,
42 (top to bottom)
Olexa/Shutterstock, zenobia_joy/
Flickr, sdewdney/iStockphoto,
zenobia_joy/Flickr,
43 Chris Hepburn/iStockphoto,
44 Alma Robinson/PA Photos/Landov

Copyright © 2011 Heinle, Cengage Learning

ALL RIGHTS RESERVED. No part of this work covered by the copyright herein may be reproduced, transmitted, stored, or used in any form or by any means graphic, electronic, or mechanical, including but not limited to photocopying, recording, scanning, digitizing, taping, Web distribution, information networks, or information storage and retrieval systems, except as permitted under Section 107 or 108 of the 1976 United States Copyright Act, without the prior written permission of the publisher.

For permission to use material from this text or product, submit all requests online at **www.cengage.com/permissions**
Further permissions questions can be emailed to
permissionrequest@cengage.com

ISBN-13: 978-1-4240-4638-6

ISBN-10: 1-4240-4638-6

Heinle
20 Channel Center Street
Boston, Massachusetts 02210
USA

Cengage Learning is a leading provider of customized learning solutions with office locations around the globe, including Singapore, the United Kingdom, Australia, Mexico, Brazil, and Japan. Locate your local office at:
international.cengage.com/region

Cengage Learning products are represented in Canada by Nelson Education, Ltd.

Visit Heinle online at **elt.heinle.com**

Visit our corporate website at
www.cengage.com

Printed in the United States of America
1 2 3 4 5 6 7 – 14 13 12 11 10

Contents

Background Reading

People in the story

Charles (Chuck) Kingston
Charles is a student at
Brenton College. He's a
business student, but his real
love is free running.

Johnny Rosa
Johnny Rosa is the leader of
the free running team.
He thinks Chuck is their best
free runner.

John Kingston
John Kingston is Charles's
father. He wants Charles
to take over his business
after college.

Ying-Chu Zhang
Ying-Chu is a good friend of
Charles. She is in the same
classes as he is.

Brent Gray
Brent Gray is a well-
known free runner from
California.

Crazy Alex
Crazy Alex is the best free
runner on the free-running
team.

This story is set in Brenton, a college town in the
northwestern United States.

Chapter 1

The replacement

"This one's easy," said Crazy Alex. The young man ran to the wall, put his hands on it, and jumped over it. He continued running as he landed on the other side of the wall.

"Maybe we need to warm up first," said Charles, but Alex wasn't listening.

Charles's full name was Charles Kingston, but most people called him Chuck. He was a very tall, thin young man. He loved free running, a sport with lots of jumping and running around the city. Free runners like to use parking garages and other places to run and jump in. They jump over walls and other things. Charles not only liked it; he was good at it, too.

Now Crazy Alex was getting ready for a big race, and Charles was helping him.

The two young men were in the parking garage of a large shopping center in Seattle. It was evening, and they were on the first floor of the parking garage. It was a good place and time to practice; there weren't many cars or people at that time of day.

"Let's go again," said Charles.

"No, I want to try that one over there," Alex said.

Alex was looking at a higher wall at the other end of the parking garage.

The race was the next evening, and it was a big one. Alex was a short man and the best free runner on the team. Charles liked to practice with him because he was so good. But sometimes he wasn't very careful when he did his jumps and runs; that's why he had the name "Crazy Alex."

"OK," said Charles. "Let's see if we can get over that one . . ."

Alex was already running fast toward it. When he got to it, he ran up the wall and jumped, catching the top of it with his hands. He pulled himself up and disappeared over the other side. Suddenly, Charles heard a cry. "Aagh!"

Charles ran over to the other side of the wall. Crazy Alex was on the ground. He was holding his ankle, and his face showed that he was hurt. "Ow," said Alex. "I can't walk."

"Well," said Johnny Rosa, the team's leader. "Alex can't run tomorrow, that's for sure." Rosa was a well-built young man of about twenty-one. He had a lot of black hair, which he put his hand through as he talked.

The team was having a meeting later that evening at the Red Door Café in downtown Seattle. There were seven of them all sitting around the table. Crazy Alex wasn't there. He was already at home, his ankle on ice.

"What are we going to do?" asked Ray Sato.

"Somebody else needs to run in the race," said Johnny Rosa. Races weren't usual because free running wasn't a competitive sport—it was more about "finding your own way." Still, some of the top free runners ran in secret races against each other.

"It's an important one," Johnny went on. "We need somebody to run there. Chuck, you're our best runner, apart from Crazy Alex . . ." Runners had to be members of a team for this race, and each team could only have one runner in each race.

"I can do it," said Charles.

Pete Jackson and the others looked at him and then looked at Johnny Rosa. "Do you have time?" asked Jane Wang, another member of the team. She smiled, but her smile wasn't friendly. "What about college?"

Charles was a business student at Brenton College. He sometimes couldn't practice with the team because he had college work.

"I don't know, Johnny," said Will Kent, turning his back to Charles. "Is he really serious about the team? He doesn't practice very much." Kent was never friendly to Charles. He seemed to really dislike him, but Charles didn't know why.

"I know the course," Charles said. "I was helping Alex to get ready for the race, remember?"

Johnny Rosa looked at Will Kent and then around the table at each member of the team. "With Alex out of it, Chuck is our best chance of winning this race," he said. "I say he does it. Now, does anybody have anything else to say?"

Nobody spoke.

Johnny Rosa said, "OK, Chuck. You're in the race."

Chapter 2

The day job

It was late when Charles got home. He opened the front door of his parents' big house in a rich part of Seattle and went quietly to his room. *Good,* he thought, *they're in bed.*

Charles went into his bedroom. He was tired and really wanted to go to sleep, but he still had some studying to do for his class the next day. He was always behind with his work.

He sat down at his desk and turned on the lamp. He opened a huge book called "Business Administration."

Very soon, the words started to dance in front of his eyes, and he found that he was thinking about his bed, not business. It was like this every time he started to study. *Is business really for me?* Charles asked himself, for the thousandth time. His eyes began to close.

"Charles?"

Charles jumped and turned around to see his father, in his pajamas, in the doorway.

John Kingston was a large man of fifty-six years. He owned a business, Kingston Electronics. The business had started small, but now it was very big. It was one of the biggest businesses in Seattle, Washington. Kingston was a kind man, but he expected others to listen to him.

"Where were you tonight?" he asked his son. He looked serious.

"In the library, Dad," said Charles. "I was studying."

"So why are you studying now?" asked his father.

"I, um . . ."

"How's your course?"

"It's fine," said Charles. "No problems."

"Really?" asked his father, walking into his son's room, "because I saw Vic De Veer on the golf course today . . ." Victor De Veer was the vice president of Brenton College. Charles didn't say anything. He was beginning to understand what his father was saying now.

"He told me that you were finding the course very difficult," said his father.

Charles looked down. His father sat down next to him.

"What is it, Charles?" asked his father. "Why exactly are you finding the course so difficult?"

"Well," Charles started. "The thing is . . . , I'm just not good at this, Dad. I think business is just not for me . . ."

John Kingston wanted his son to take over Kingston Electronics. "Not for you?" he said. "Of course it's for you!" Charles's father sat down next to him. "Listen to me, son. You just need to get through the course. I know you're not the number one student. I know you're not . . ." His father stopped talking and turned his face away.

Not Peter, thought Charles. *You wanted to say I'm not Peter, didn't you?*

Peter was Charles's big brother. The plan was always for Peter to take over the family business. Peter had loved business. The problem was that Peter was dead. Three years ago, Peter died in a car accident. Charles and his father never talked about Peter. Now Charles was his father's hope for the future of his business.

"Look, I had an idea, Charles," said his father, standing up. "We can bring in someone to help."

"What sort of help?"

"Your mother and I talked. We've got you a personal tutor, who will come here to the house to help you study. His name is Mr. Baldwin. He's one of the best, I hear."

Charles looked at his father in surprise.

"Starting tomorrow evening at 7:30," his father went on.

"Dad, I . . . That's difficult . . ."

"Why?"

Charles didn't know what to say. He couldn't tell him about the race.

"Don't worry, son. Believe me, I won't let you fail. You and me, we'll get through this together."

Chapter 3

Getting to the race

Charles didn't sleep well that night. He couldn't stop thinking. A personal tutor! His father was very upset earlier on. Charles could see that, and he didn't want to make his father unhappy. But what about the race? It was tomorrow evening at 7:00.

The next morning, Charles went into the kitchen to get some coffee. His mother, Mary, was there. "You look tired, Charles," she said. "Were you up all night studying?"

Charles didn't reply.

"I'm sure the tutor will help you with your studies," his mother said. She talked to him for a while. When she was young, his mother was a very fast runner. She nearly became a professional, but then she met Charles's father and had children. *Peter was like Dad, and I'm like Mom,* he thought. Charles thought about talking to her about his problem, but he didn't want to talk about Peter to her. They never talked about Peter. It was too hard.

I have to phone Johnny, Charles thought. What was he going to say to him after yesterday evening? Johnny was really helping him.

"OK, Mom," he said, leaving the kitchen. "I'll see you later."

On the way to college, Charles phoned Johnny and told him about his father and the tutor. "I'm sorry," he said. "I know you tried to help me . . ."

"Well," said Johnny, "you have to find a way, Chuck. Just make sure that you're at the race!"

"Listen, Johnny, I'm sorry, but . . ."

"Chuck, you've got to make a decision now. Do you want to be part of this team or don't you?"

"Of course I do, Johnny. You know that."

"Then be there tonight."

The phone went quiet.

◇◇◇

Charles went to his business class. He remembered reading something last night. *What was it again?* He asked himself. He felt very tired, and found it hard to listen to the teacher, Ms. Yamin. His eyes began to close, then . . .

"What do you think about that, Charles?" Ms. Yamin asked him.

Charles's eyes opened. "I . . . um . . . ," he said.

A few students laughed, but not Ms. Yamin.

After the class, his friend Ying-Chu came up to him.

"Let's go for coffee," she said. She was studying economics, but as part of her course, she had to take one or two courses in business. Charles liked her; she was good to talk to, and they often had coffee together after class. They walked to Ben's Café.

"So what is it, Chuck?" she asked as they sat down with their coffee. "You don't look too good!"

Charles told her about the personal tutor and the race.

"Didn't you tell your dad about the race?"

"My dad doesn't even know that I *do* free running," Charles replied.

"Really? Why don't you tell him?" asked Ying-Chu.

"I don't know. I thought about it. But I think he'll be really upset. He wants me to really do well in college, and then . . . he wants me to take over the family business. Just like Peter. I can't tell him that I don't really want to do it. It'll break his heart."

Ying-Chu looked at Charles. She knew about Peter's death. "So what are you going to do?"

"That's just it," said Charles. "I don't know . . ." He told her about the call with Johnny Rosa. ". . . I *have* to go," he finished. "If I don't go, they won't want me on the team."

"But isn't free running just what you do in your free time?" she asked. "What about your studies? What about your future? You have to think about the future, Chuck!"

"That's what my mom and dad say," said Charles. "I know that business is good for my future, but what I really love is free running. I feel so good when I do it!"

"Well, I can see that!" she said, and smiled. She thought for a minute. Then she said. "Why don't you phone the tutor and try to make the class earlier? Then you can go to the race after the class!"

"I don't have the number. And I can't ask my father, can I?"

Ying-Chu thought for a moment, then got up and asked the waitress for something. A moment later, she came back with a phone book. "What's that for?" Charles asked.

"We can get his number from here. The tutor, I mean. What's the name?"

"Um, let me think," Charles closed his eyes. "Bald . . . Baldy . . ."

"Baldy?!"

"Baldwin! His name's Baldwin." Ying-Chu looked through the book.

"Here! *Mr. G.T. Baldwin. Business and Economics Tutoring.* That's him, right?"

"That's him, all right."

Charles took out his phone and called the number.

◇◇◇

Charles hurried home from college. His class with Mr. Baldwin was at 5:30 now. *An hour for the class*, he thought, *then I get ready to go to the race.* The race started at 7:00, so he could be there in time.

Mr. Baldwin sat down with Charles and started to talk about business law. Charles watched the clock over his desk. He tried to understand the tutor, but it was very difficult. At 6:15, Mr. Baldwin said, "I'm not leaving until you understand this, Charles."

He said it in a kind voice; he was letting Charles know that he planned to help him. But Charles looked at the clock and thought, *Oh no!* He tried to listen to what Mr. Baldwin was saying.

In the end, Charles's class didn't finish until after seven o'clock. He tried to phone to tell them he was coming, but he couldn't get through. Charles hurried to the place where the race was, but it was too late. The race was finished when he got there.

◇◇◇

The next evening, Charles went to meet the team as usual. Only Crazy Alex was missing. His ankle was still in a bad way.

"I'm sorry, guys," Charles said.

Johnny didn't speak.

"So what happened?" asked Ray Sato.

"Yeah!" said Jane Wang. "Why didn't you race, Chuck?"

All the members of the team were angry with Charles.

"I'm sorry," said Charles. "I had a problem at home."

"What kind of problem?"

Charles had to tell them. "My dad," he said. "He kind of made me study . . ."

"Your dad made you study?" said Ray Sato, laughing. "Are you serious?"

Will Kent wasn't laughing. "He can't stay on the team, Johnny," he said. "Chuck's good, but he's not serious about this. He's not right for the team." Two or three of the others agreed with Will Kent.

"Johnny?" said Will Kent.

Johnny Rosa listened and looked round the team. Then he looked at Charles. "They're right," he said. "You're out, Chuck."

Chapter 4

A difficult course

Charles left the meeting, but he didn't go home. He waited for Johnny Rosa in the parking lot. Half an hour later, the meeting finished and Johnny came out. Charles waited for the others to go. Then he walked up to him.

"What do you want, Chuck?" asked Johnny.

"Give me another chance," Charles said. "Please . . ."

"Chuck, I like you. I really do," said Johnny Rosa. "And you're a good runner. But the guys are right. You're not serious."

"I . . ." Charles started. "Listen, I need to tell you something."

"What?" said Johnny.

Charles told him about his brother, and how his father wanted him to be like his brother and run the family business for him.

"Hey, I'm sorry. I didn't know, Chuck," said Johnny Rosa.

"That's why it's so difficult for me," said Charles.

Johnny Rosa looked at Charles. "But you still want to race?"

"More than anything," said Charles.

"Listen," Johnny said. "There's another big race on Sunday. It's a really big one here in Seattle. Difficult competition, but really good money for the winner."

"I'll do it," said Charles.

"And Chuck . . . ," Johnny Rosa said.

Charles looked at him. "Yes, Johnny?"

"Make sure that you get there and win this time."

◇◇◇

Charles didn't have much time to get ready for the race. On Friday afternoon, he didn't go to class. He didn't know the route that the race took through the city, and he wanted to practice it.

The race started at an empty building lot on the edge of downtown. The sun was warm. Charles started practicing the run, jumping from wall to wall. As soon as he started running and jumping, he felt free, happier than he had felt for days. He lost himself, forgetting his worries as he felt the ground, walls, steps. Very soon, he was near the end of the course. Just before the end there was a big wall. Charles always had trouble with walls—he was good at running and jumping, but not so good at climbing walls. And this one was *big*.

He stopped, and looked at the wall carefully, thinking about it.

Then he saw another man near the wall, a young blond man with a face made brown by the sun. The man just sat there. Charles knew him from somewhere.

"Hey," said Chuck.

"Hey," the young man said.

"Don't I know you?" Charles asked.

"I don't know," the young man said. "Do you?"

Suddenly Charles remembered. The young man was Brent Gray, a well-known free runner from California. He remembered seeing his face in the free-running magazines—he was very famous.

"You're Brent Gray," Charles said. "I'm Chuck. It's great to meet you."

Brent Gray smiled at him.

"You've got some good moves there," said Gray.

"Hey, thanks," Charles said. "I'm just getting ready for the race this Sunday. Are you running?"

"Sure."

Brent Gray in the race, thought Charles. *That is going to make it even more difficult!*

"Did you do this yet?" Charles asked, looking at the wall.

"No," Gray said.

Charles smiled. The two of them went over to the wall and looked at it.

"About two and a half meters?" Charles said.

"Nearer to three," said Gray.

I've never climbed one this high, thought Charles, but he didn't say anything to Gray.

Charles ran up to the wall, jumped off his left foot, put his right foot on the wall, and jumped again. His hands missed the top, and he dropped back down.

"That's really high," said Gray.

Gray tried next. It was hard for him, but he got over.

"I need to practice that one," said Charles.

"You'll get it," said Gray. "Sit down for a few minutes and have a rest."

The two young men sat down.

"Are you a professional?" Gray asked Charles.

"No . . . I just like it."

"I'm surprised. You're very good; you could think about going professional."

"I'm sure it's very difficult."

"Well, maybe," said Gray. "The money from the races isn't so good, as you know. There are modeling jobs. I get work in movies now sometimes—you know, as a stuntman. Some of us even have sponsors—I get paid for wearing these clothes."

"But you have to be good, right?" Charles said.

Gray smiled.

"It's not just that. You've got to look after yourself," said Gray. "A lot of guys I know—they weren't careful enough and now they're finished. They've got bad ankles, bad backs. I'm still doing it because I'm careful."

Charles thought about Crazy Alex, then said, "Why did you become a free runner?"

"I love it, that's all," Gray smiled. "But it wasn't easy. I was studying to be a lawyer. Can you believe that? But my heart wasn't in it."

My heart wasn't in it, thought Charles. That was a good way to say what he, Charles, felt about business . . .

◇◇◇

Charles was at the wall for three hours. Later, he told Ying-Chu about his afternoon.

"So did you climb the wall?" she asked.

"I got it in the end. There was another runner there. He helped me with it."

He told her about his practice, and about Brent Gray.

"Really?" Ying-Chu's eyes were big. "I had no idea there were professionals."

"Free running is normal these days," he said, "and a lot of people do it. But I didn't know you could get so much work."

"It sounds a little dangerous, Chuck!" she said. "I don't know why you can't just go running, like me." Ying-Chu loved running, and people often saw her running around the campus.

"Well," said Charles, "it *can* be dangerous. You have to be careful . . ."

"So you think you can really *be* a free runner?" asked Ying-Chu. "Make money at it and everything?"

"Only the very best can do that," said Charles, "like Brent Gray. But even then, it's not easy. I know that."

"Well, it sounds like you have to make a decision," said Ying-Chu. "I mean if you really want to be good at it, like this Gray guy . . ."

"I love it, Ying-Chu," said Charles. "When I'm running and jumping, I feel great, you know. I feel . . ." Charles thought about it for a moment. ". . . free. That's how I feel. I feel free."

Ying-Chu looked at Charles carefully.

"It sounds to me," she said, "like you already know what to do."

Chapter 5

Rain

Twenty young men lined up at the start of the race on Sunday afternoon. It was raining hard, as it often rained in Seattle. *I have to be careful in this rain*, thought Charles, *because the ground is wet.* He was already thinking about the big wall at the end of the race. He knew that he was slow, and he knew that Brent Gray could climb it easily.

Brent Gray was standing next to Charles. *Good luck*, Brent smiled at Charles. Charles also saw some young men standing in the crowd. Charles knew they were sponsors, even though they didn't look like it. Sponsors of free running were usually young and really big fans of the sport.

Still, Crazy Alex and Johnny Rosa were there, though Alex still couldn't walk very well. And there was Ying-Chu, and some of his college friends, too. She waved at him. "Come on, Chuck!" she called. It was good to see them all. *I hope I run a good race*, Charles thought.

"Go!" The race started, and Charles and Brent Gray very soon went into the lead. It was just between the two of them for the first part of the race, and soon the rest of the runners were well behind. It rained and rained and rained. Very soon Charles was very wet. But he ran and jumped well, and he was with Gray through the beginning and the middle of the race.

Coming to the last part of the race, Charles was winning. But then there was the wall. This was the big test for Charles. Could he get over it quickly? He felt Gray behind him.

He ran at the wall and jumped, but his hands missed the top.

No! thought Charles.

Gray ran past him, jumped up, and climbed over the wall.

This time I must do it, Charles thought.

He ran up to the wall and jumped again. This time, his feet found the top. But the wall was slippery.

I can do it! Charles thought, pulling himself up.

Then he was over. When he dropped down the other side of the wall, Gray was just a few meters in front of him!

I did it, thought Charles. Now he had to catch the Californian! He had to win! He ran as hard as he could and used all his skill to jump and run around the rest of the course. *The finish line can't be far away,* thought Charles. Gray was just a few meters in front of him now!

Charles ran hard. He could see the finish line. He could see Ying-Chu, Alex, and Johnny shouting, "Come on, Chuck!" He felt like he couldn't run any faster, but somehow he did. Now he was next to Brent Gray. Then, little by little, Charles went past the Californian. The finish line was just there. Charles made one last push for the line. Yes! He was the winner.

"Chuck, you won!" called Ying-Chu as she and the others came round Charles. Charles was very tired. But he was smiling, a really big smile.

Then he heard someone say, "Charles, what *is* this?!"

Charles turned around to see his father.

Chapter 6

Running free

"I knew it! I knew there was something!" Charles's father was shouting. "Vic De Veer told me. A son of mine, failing a business course! I knew you were doing something stupid!"

Charles and his father were driving home.

"So you followed me?" Charles asked.

"Don't even speak to me, Charles!"

They didn't speak again until they got home.

Mary Kingston was in the living room, waiting for them. John Kingston told her about the free-running race. ". . . and that's where I found him," he finished. He was so angry that he walked around the living room as he spoke.

"This is what I want to do, Dad. This is what I love," said Charles.

"Love?" shouted his father. "What about your studies? It's crazy, Charles, it really is!"

"It isn't crazy, Dad," Charles said. His voice was serious. "It's what I want to do."

"What you want to do?" asked his father. "What about the family business?"

"I don't *want* to run the family business, Dad," said Charles. As he said it, Charles felt lighter somehow. He looked at his mother. She didn't look surprised.

"I . . . what? What about what we want, your mother and I?" his father said. "Why, I've never heard such . . . You listen to me, boy. If you continue with this 'free running' thing of yours, well, then you're no son of mine!"

Charles's mother looked surprised.

"Oh, John . . ." she said.

John Kingston sat down. His face was white.

"'No son of mine?' This isn't about free running at all, is it, Dad? It's about Peter."

"What?" his father said.

"It is, isn't it? You want me to be like Peter, don't you? Well, I'm not, Dad! I never was and I never will be."

Charles was crying now. But he went on, "It was always like this, too. You always said to Peter, 'You're your father's son.' You always said that. But never to me, Dad."

John Kingston looked up at his son. "I . . ." They never talked about Peter, and hearing his name was difficult for all of them.

"I always loved you both," he said.

Charles's mother went to her husband and put her arm around him. "I know you did, John," she said softly. "But Charles is right. He has to go his own way."

"I don't want to hurt you," Charles went on. He was looking at both of them. "But this is what I want to do. Please understand that."

Now his father was upset, Charles could see.

"But the business," John said. "I built this business for all of us. To give it to you, my sons . . ."

"It will be OK," said Mary Kingston to her husband. "It's your love that you give your son, John. Not the business. The business will be fine. When you stop working, you can sell it. Isn't it more important that your son is happy?"

John Kingston looked at his wife and held her hand.

"I know you want me to be good at business," Charles said, in a soft voice. "But I'm not. Peter was really good. But I'm me, and I can't run the family business. I just can't . . ."

"But what will you do, Charles?" his father asked him.

"I want to take a year off my studies, do free running seriously. I'll try to become a professional."

John Kingston listened. He didn't look angry anymore.

Charles walked over to his father.

"I miss Peter, too, Dad," he said.

Charles's mother and father put their arms around their son, and the three of them held each other.

"I know you do, son," his father said. "I know you do."

A few days later, Charles and Ying-Chu were sitting in a café in the town, drinking coffee and talking. He told her about what had happened at home after the race.

"So, what are you going to do?" she asked him.

"Well," he said, "take a year off and see if I really like free running, you know? And if I can make money at it . . ."

"And your father?" Ying-Chu asked.

"We had a long talk," Charles said. "He'll be OK with it. We talked about a lot of things, about Peter. It's better now."

He looked away for a moment, remembering. Then he smiled.

"What's the big smile about?" she asked.

Charles took out a piece of paper from his bag.

"What's that?" asked Ying-Chu.

"A phone number of a sponsor," Charles replied. "They called me after they saw me win the race. They want me to talk to them. Shall I call them?"

Ying-Chu smiled at him and gave him her phone. "What are you waiting for?" she asked.

Review

A. Match the characters in the story to their descriptions.

1. _____ Chuck Kingston
2. _____ Johnny Rosa
3. _____ Ying-Chu
4. _____ Brent Gray
5. _____ Crazy Alex
6. _____ John Kingston

a. a famous free runner from California
b. a free runner on Chuck's team who got injured
c. Chuck's friend and classmate
d. the leader of Chuck's free running team
e. a successful businessman
f. a business student at Brenton College and a free runner

B. Complete each sentence with the correct word from the box.

sponsor	ankle	decision	professional
business	tutor	accident	serious

1. A _____ is a special kind of teacher.

2. A _____ is someone who does an activity for money rather than as a hobby.

3. Your _____ is the part of your body that joins your foot and your leg.

4. _____ is work that is related to producing, buying, and selling things.

5. If you are _____ about something, you really mean what you say or do.

6. A _____ is a person or organization that pays for an event or person.

7. When you make a _____, you choose what to do.

8. If someone has an _____, something bad happens to them by chance.

C. Choose the best answer for each question.

1. Why does Charles take part in the first race?

  a. He had to replace his injured teammate.

  b. His team members forced him to take part.

  c. He wants to show his father how good he is.

2. What is the main reason for Charles studying business at Brenton?

  a. His dream is to take over the family business.

  b. His father wants him to take over the family business.

  c. He knows he doesn't have a future as a free runner.

3. Why do the other members in the team dislike Charles?

  a. They feel he is not serious about being a free runner.

  b. They feel he is not good enough to be on their team.

  c. They are jealous because he comes from a rich family.

4. What lesson does Charles NOT learn from Brent Gray?

  a. He should learn to follow his heart.

  b. He should be careful when he trains.

  c. He should learn new free running tricks.

5. Charles thinks the real reason his father wants him to study business is because he _____.

  a. does not want to sell the family business

  b. thinks free running is a dangerous sport

  c. wants Charles to be more like his brother Peter

D. Write the name of the character who said the words.

1. "I was studying to be a lawyer. Can you believe that? But my heart wasn't in it." ____________

2. "I know you want me to be good at business. But I'm not. Peter was really good. But I'm me, and I can't run the family business." ______________

3. "Why don't you phone the tutor and try to make the class earlier? Then you can go to the race after class!" ______________

4. "You've got to make a decision now. Do you want to be part of this team or don't you?" ______________

5. "You listen to me, boy. If you continue with this 'free running' thing of yours, well, then you're no son of mine!" ______________

Charles Kingston

Crazy Alex

John Kingston

Brent Gray

Ying-Chu Zhang

Answer Key

A: 1. f; 2. d; 3. c; 4. a; 5. b; 6. e

B: 1. tutor; 2. professional; 3. ankle; 4. business; 5. serious; 6. sponsor; 7. decision; 8. accident

C: 1. a; 2. b; 3. a; 4. b; 5. c

D: 1. Brent Gray; 2. Charles Kingston; 3. Ying-Chu; 4. Johnny Rosa; 5. Mary Kingston

Background Reading:

Spotlight on . . .
Parkour and Free Running

Free running and parkour (French for "the art of moving") are extreme sports which are becoming more popular with urban youth. They are art forms of human movement similar to martial arts or dancing.

The people who practice them are called traceurs. Their aim is to move over, under, around, and through obstacles (both man-made and natural) around them. Such movement may come in the form of running, jumping, climbing, and other more complex techniques.

What do I need?

The great thing about free running is that it doesn't cost a lot of money, but you do need a fit and healthy body, a willingness to learn, and an open mind.

How do I start?

For beginners, try and find a group in your area with experienced people who can teach you. You can also find videos on the Internet which demonstrate the different moves. The sport is becoming more popular, and there may even be a special school for it in your city!

Tic-tac

What are some basic moves I should know?

Roll: Keep your knees bent and do a forward roll as you land to soften the fall.

This is the most important move in free running, as landing properly can save you from serious injury.

Cat leap: Jump toward the object and land with your feet first against the wall, then grab the wall with your hands and pull yourself up and over it. This move is used to climb over high walls.

Speed vault: A fast way of getting past low obstacles. Jump over an obstacle by swinging your legs to one side, using your hands to support yourself.

Tic tac: This move is great when for corners or when you need to gain height to grab something. Run toward the wall and kick off of it in order to get to the adjacent wall.

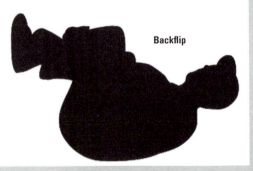

Backflip

I heard parkour/free running is very dangerous. How do I stay safe?

Any sport can be dangerous if you're not prepared. The most important rule is to know your limits. Beginners should work in groups and train with experienced traceurs. Practice your moves on something soft first and always be aware of your surroundings. Free running involves a lot of hard work and is not about crazy moves or rooftop jumps. The stunts you see on TV are done by people with years and years of experience!

What's the difference between parkour and free running?

They may share the same moves but they actually have very different principles. Parkour focuses on moving quickly from one point to another. Free running is more about freedom of movement—the moves tend to be more experimental and creative.

Backflip with straight legs

Background Reading:
Spotlight on ... *Sébastien Foucan*

Date of birth: 24 May 1974
Nationality: French (his parents are from Guadeloupe, in the Caribbean)
Family: Married with two children

Sébastien Foucan is the founder of free running, and also one of the world's best-known parkour runners. Most people recognize him for his role in the opening scenes of the James Bond movie *Casino Royale*. He's also been featured in documentaries on parkour like *Jump Britain* and *Jump London*, and has even gone on tour with Madonna as one of her dancers!

Jump

After practicing parkour for many years, Sébastien decided to follow his own path. Along the way, he became very interested in martial arts, particularly the work of Bruce Lee, and developed free running as a way to express himself through movement. Now, he travels the world and has published a book to promote his sport. He has even started a free running school for people who are truly interested in learning his art.

The Free Running Philosophy

No violence – Focus on passion and creativity.
No competition – The journey is more important than the goal.
No group – We are all different; find your own path.
No chief – Follow your way; let no one lead you.

"Not everybody can be a champion, but the most important thing is that you can try."

Sébastien Foucan

Think About It

1. Think of other sports or disciplines which involve free expression of ideas.

2. How do you think free runners train?

Running

Glossary

ankle	(*n.*)	a part of your foot
climb	(*v.*)	When you climb a mountain, you go from the bottom to the top.
competition	(*n.*)	when two or more people try to win a prize
decision	(*n.*)	a choice to do something
drop	(*v.*)	to fall to the ground from a high place
edge	(*n.*)	the side of something
fail	(*v.*)	to do badly, not pass a test
hurt	(*v.*)	You can hurt yourself if you fall off your bike.
land	(*v.*)	You land on the ground when your feet touch the ground after jumping.
practice	(*v.*)	to try something again and again to get better at it
professional	(*adj. and n.*)	someone who is paid money, such as a sportsperson
race	(*v. and n.*)	When two or more people race, they try to go the fastest for a certain distance.
slippery	(*adj.*)	When the ground is wet, it is slippery and you may fall.
sponsor	(*n.*)	someone who pays professionals to play sports
stuntman	(*n.*)	a person who does dangerous things in a movie
tutor	(*n.*)	a private teacher
upset	(*adj.*)	unhappy or sad because something bad happened